When you open a book,
You open a door,
Which opens your mind,
To expanding it more.

- Susan A. Turfle

Keep Feeding Your Spark

A Collection of Children's Poems to Nurture
Critical Thinking, Curiosity, Gratitude and Humor

by

Susan A. Turfle

MakingRipplesPublishing.com

Copyright © 2021 by Making Ripples Publishing, LLC.
Illustration copyright © 2021 by Making Ripples Publishing, LLC.
Cover copyright © 2021 by Making Ripples Publishing, LLC.

All rights reserved. No part of this book may be reproduced, stored in a retrieval system or transmitted in any form or by any means, electronic, mechanical, photocopying, recording, or otherwise or used in any manner whatsoever without the prior express written permission of the copyright owner except for the use of quotations in a book review.

First hardback edition November 2021
Book design by Susan A. Turfle

ISBN: 979-8-9852783-0-9

Published in the United States of America by
Making Ripples Publishing, LLC.

SusanATurfle.com

This book is dedicated to Turf, my husband. I am thankful that you never outwardly discourage my creative endeavors and my need to dream in vivid color.

In the past, you vented my kiln, built me a sturdy workbench, ran extra lighting, listened to me hammering metals in the middle of the night, built forms so that I could acid stain concrete and overlooked spilled paint on the floor. I do hope that you find my writing and doodlestrations to be a much less intrusive adventure.

I am deeply grateful that we are holding each other's hand on this wild ride together.

FORGETFUL OSTRICH

Exactly how
        do birds really fly?
I think to myself
        as I look at the sky,

Covered in feathers
        from their tails to their beaks,
Slicing thru air
        while leaving no streaks,

I'm told it's related
        to thrust and to lift,
Adjusting their wings
        catching air as they drift,

High in the sky
        some fly with each other,
While some are alone
        they dart and they hover,

Birds are all over
        far and nearby,
But not all are lucky
        some can't touch the sky,

The ostrich is one bird
        that sticks to the ground,
Flying no longer
        they just run around,

This long-legged bird
        shares a lesson therefore,
If you don't use your gifts
        you'll forget how to soar.

KEEP FEEDING YOUR SPARK

Wake up I say,
Wake up sleepyhead,

Throw off your covers,
Get up out of bed,

Stretch and breathe deep,
Put your feet on the floor,

It's time to get dressed,
And walk to your door,

All that's outside,
Is not what it seems,

There's more to the light,
Than just the sun's beams,

Vibrations abound,
At various heights,

Like the ups and downs,
Of keys as one types,

So much knowledge,
Yet to discover,

Just open your door,
Then open another,

Learn all you can,
Make your own mark,

Stand in the light,
Keep feeding your spark.

MONSTERS

We've bed sheet monsters in our home,
During the night they freely roam.

In winter cold and summer heat,
They move the bed sheet to my feet.

Every dawn when the sun shines in,
Yes - that sheet's at my feet again.

No one knows how they play this trick,
Or why it's me on which they pick.

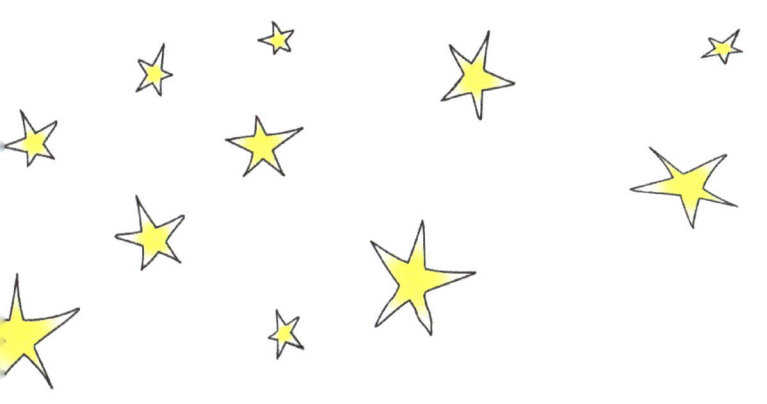

THE COLLECTOR

I know a person
>with multiple pockets,

A collector of things
>like marbles and rockets,

Has four in his pants
>and his jacket has two,

He picks all things up
>like his fingers are glue,

In those deep pockets
>he stores them away,

Filling them up
>each day after day,

Carrying around
>the possessions he's found,

Keeps him quite heavy
>attached to the ground,

Shoving more in
      he hopes all will fit,

Walks very slowly
      he complains quite a bit,

Never has thought
      to lighten his load,

Or if comes a day
      his seams will explode,

Being weighed down
      doesn't seem like much fun,

I'd rather be light
      more able to run,

Jumping so high
      spreading my wings,

I refuse to collect
      and carry those things.

BLUE BEES

Lean your head back
      with your chin towards the sky,
Always ask questions
      you can start with the why,

Why are some bees
      born to be blue?
Most wear black
      and a yellowish hue,

What is another
      question to think,
What do they eat
      and what do they drink?

Keep asking more
      and the truth you will own,
Where do they fly
      when they want to go home?

Blue bees are rare
      though there are a few types,
Some look metallic
      while others wear stripes,

Do your own research
      learn if you dare,
All of the answers
      to why, what and where.

ME AND PEAS

Me and peas have history,
I don't like them,
And they don't like me,

Served with dinner on my plate,
Big mountain of green,
A vegetable date,

It's not their scent or their taste,
Just too much work,
And my time they waste,

Roly-polies want to flee,
Peas on my spoon,
Staring back at me,

Slow and calm up to my mouth,
One always jumps,
Escaping due south,

Whizzing by next to my knee,
Hitting the floor,
I frown at that pea,

The meal goes on and it grows,
A heap of peas,
Right next to my toes,

Until now that's been the case,
But the time has come,
To put peas in their place,

Laughter grows inside my head,
Each thinks it's free,
But sadly mislead,

In a flash comes my new pup,
Loves eating peas,
She gobbles them up.

MOM'S DAY OFF

My mom wakes up
      with a smile on her face,
Claiming today is one day
      that she'll skip the rat race,

No driving to work
      she's relaxing at home,
To catch up with friends
      and play on her phone,

I hug her goodbye
      as I head out the door,
Then she slowly bends down
      and squints at the floor,

It's dirty she thinks
      as she hunts for the mop,
Says once that's all done
      on the couch I will plop,

With the third load of laundry
      folded up neat,
She thinks to herself
      I'll shop while I eat,

She looks up from her screen
      to see a few crumbs,
So she scrubs all the counters
      as she grins and she hums,

Both bathrooms need cleaning
        and in no time at all,
She's finished with those
        and heads straight down the hall,

With a duster in one hand
        she shakes out each rug,
But what's for dinner
        gives her mind a quick tug,

She heads to the fridge
        and opens the doors,
Starts chopping up veggies
        and in a pot gently pours,

Some stock to make soup
        with fresh bread on the side,
She takes a step back
        grinning with pride,

As I walk through the door
        my gut loudly rumbles,
"What time is dinner?"
        from my mouth quickly tumbles,

"How was your day off?"
        I ask while we eat,
Sitting back, she laughs
        as she rubs her sore feet.

SOMETIMES I KNOW

Sometimes I feel
      like my head is too tight,

Should I go left
      should I go right,

Sometimes I want
      everything that I see,

What others possess
      may not be for me,

Sometimes I think
      this race is too fast,

Many seem worried
      of finishing last,

Sometimes I take
      a moment to breathe,

Clearing my thoughts
      peace to receive,

Sometimes I know
      I am all that I need,

Open my mind
      listen and heed.

GRANDPA'S OLD BONES

My grandpa owns
      many noisy things,
Some held together
      with tape and with strings,

I am close to him
      he means more to me,
Than many of those
      whom I frequently see.

His reading glasses
      with the black wire frames,
Are old like me
      he cheerfully claims,

They creak a bit
      when he puts them on,
The sound is there
      and then it is gone.

When he gently drops down
      in his overstuffed chair,
I hear moans and groans
      from I don't know where,

The noises continue
      when he shifts around,
His furniture makes
      an unusual sound.

He takes tiny steps
        when he walks to the door,
His shoes crackle softly
        as they shuffle the floor,

Though he moves steady
        with the use of his cane,
You clearly can tell
        it's a bit of a strain.

He tells me stories
        sitting at his table,
Great days of fishing
        when he was more able,

The cup he uses
        makes a snapping sound,
After he sips
        and while placing it down.

His glasses, his chair,
        his shoes and his cup,
Are just a few things
        from which noises erupt,

As I ponder these things
        that make creaks and groans,
I'm wondering now
        if it's grandpa's old bones.

INNER CHILD

Grow that space inside your head,
Expand a little more,
Upside down or inside out,
Continue to explore.

Exercise your inner child,
Try each and every day,
For if you let them rest too long,
They may just go away.

Your inner child is deep within,
Curious as can be,
Being born with special eyes,
From which only they can see.

The world to them is a boundless place,
That may not look like ours,
They help us see what it can be,
To live among the stars.

It's like looking through a magic lens,
Not one that has a blur,
For in their world most anything,
Really can occur.

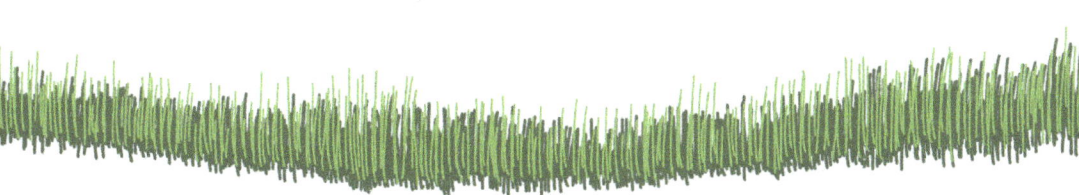

DECISIONS

Today you may find
      it's a wonderful day,

All that you do
      seems to go your own way,

Yet moments will come
      when things are not right,

It's those in between times
      like the sun is too bright,

You might feel a slight tug
      trying to pull you one way,

But it may not be best
      and in thoughts it will weigh,

Many choices will come
      and you'll learn to decide,

The best path for you
      and to set others aside.

KITES

Kites are fun
        when they kiss the sun,

Until their tether
        floats down like a feather,

Watching it fly
        I mumble goodbye.

WHISPERING TREES

Do you know
    trees speak to each other?
Secretly whispering
    to their sister and brother,

Helping each other
    signals are sent,
Straight through their roots
    and by air with a scent,

Trees are not simple
    though they may seem,
Only to bend
    towards the sun's brightest beam,

Working together
    in sync like a dance,
Their language is quiet
    overlooked at a glance,

So upon a tree trunk
    go rest your bare ear,
For one never knows
    what whispers you'll hear.

ILLUSIONS

You are you,
I am me,

We are more,
Than what we see,

Make no assumptions,
Or trust their conclusions,

Investigate fully,
Rise above all illusions.

TANGLED

Wires, wires -
      everywhere,
Some are here
      and some are there,
To plug in phones
      and charge laptops,
Handheld games
      it doesn't stop,
Giving power
      to all this stuff,
More and more
      is not enough,
Take the time
      to raise your chin,
From the screen
      you're tangled in,
Speak with words
      and do not type,
Take a break
      from all the hype,
Rise up now
      hold your face up high,
Look each other
      in the eye,
Mother, father,
      sister, brother,
Let's sit and talk
      with one another,
Friends and family
      pay high prices,
When we're trapped
      by our devices.

MY BACKPACK

I only carry
      what school requires,
Lists from my teachers
      display their desires,

Colored pencils and pens
      a yellow highlighter,
A few things I need
      to be good a writer,

Notebooks and folders
      in every hue,
Twelve erasers in pink
      and three glue sticks in blue,

One pad of paper
      in my three-ring binder,
Square sticky notes
      to write a reminder,

A pair of scissors
      a twelve-inch ruler,
My nine-zippered backpack
      couldn't be cooler,

Composition books
      in black and white,
I only need five
      in which to write,

One spiral bound notebook
      for every class,
Calculator for science
      to figure out mass,

I play the flute
>   which doesn't fit,
So in my right hand
>   I carry it,

My left hand carries
>   a lunch box flowered,
Kid strength is how
>   this whole thing is powered,

It's the first day of school
>   and I feel quite ready,
A bit shaky I am
>   my mom keeps me steady,

I'm not nervous or scared
>   but can't take a step,
I have what I need
>   I've done all my prep,

Oh why can't I go
>   oh what must it be?
I guess it's my backpack
>   it weighs more than me.

ONE RESTFUL MOMENT

My eyes are closed
        and body outstretched,
The perfect day
        in my mind has been etched,

Both feet are sore
        my muscles are tired,
A bit of peace
        now is required,

Blades of green grass
        poke at my neck,
This one restful moment
        nothing will wreck,

The sun's heat and light
        spread over my face,
While minutes of time
        have slowed down their pace,

I am still as a stone
        I listen and smell,
Breathing so softly
        as though under a spell,

Worn but content
        the day's nearly done,
I'm happy we live
        underneath our old sun.

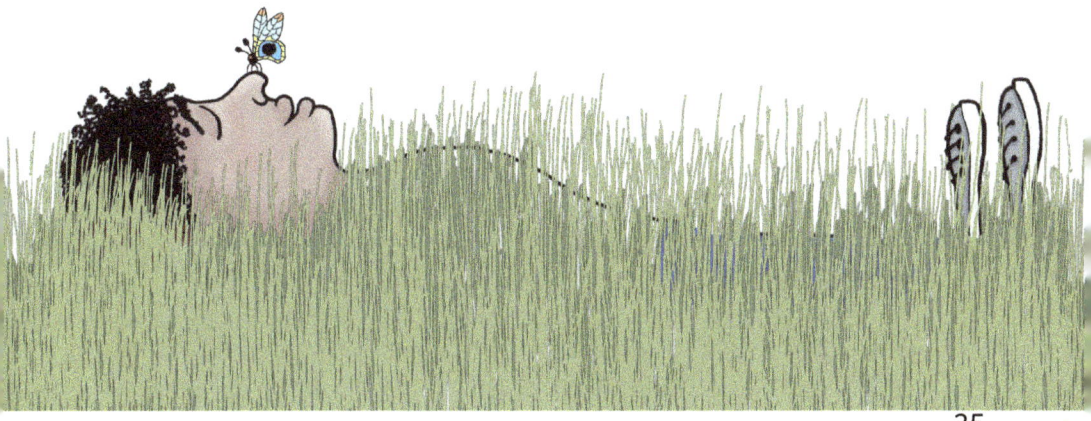

STANDING PANTS

My pants can stand
      in a room by themselves,

They're as stiff as a board
      and reek of odd smells,

Each pair is clean
      when I pick them out,

But a few drops of syrup
      dribble out of the spout,

Off of my waffles
      and onto my thigh,

You can't really tell
      I'm sure it will dry,

Then outside to play
      they get a bit grimy,

I found a few snails
      they're always real slimy,

Wiping my hands
      straight down my front pockets,

I guess that squished
      those melting milk chocolates,

I roll down a hill
      so they're covered in dirt,

The front and the back
      and also my shirt,

Poking street tar
      with a stick while it's hot,

Tar on both knees
      without any thought,

Hungry again
      I know I will score,

A meal in a bag
      when I reach the back door,

Mom hands me lunch
      a stuffed sandwich for me,

I eat it quite promptly
      sitting under a tree,

After my break
      I slowly stand up,

Knowing what dripped
      on my lap was ketchup,

Friends get together
      enjoying some ball,

Grass stains of course
      when I slide and I fall,

I'm called in for dinner
      but need a quick shower,

Clean clothes at the table
      or Mom's mood will be sour,

The measure of whether
      you've had fun I must say,

Is if your pants can stand alone
      at the end of the day.

A WONDERFUL BEAST

An elephant is
	such a wonderful beast,
Upon our great lands
	it's the largest not least,
A trunk that is used
	for eating and work,
It sits just above
	where it laughs with a smirk.

They hear with large ears
    but also with feet,
The pads on the bottom
    can sense a strange beat,
Speaking to others
    they stomp on the ground,
Feeling vibrations
    as though they are sound.

A small eye is set
    on each side of its head,
Seeing yellows and blues
    but barely a red,
All babies are blind
    though never alone,
When each is born
    a party is thrown.

The herd gathers tightly
    to celebrate birth,
Trumpeting loudly
    to the ends of the earth,
Overwhelmed with joy
    you may see them cry,
Emotions are felt
    each low and each high.

All are protective
    fulfilling their part,
Supporting each other
    with care in their heart,
The herds are made up
    of family and friends,
Loving each other
    from beginnings to ends.

CUPBOARD

Our lives
      are like a cupboard,
It's a perfect
      analogy,
Empty in
      the early days,
Shelves bare
      and clutter free,
As time moves on
      we bring things home,
And in the cupboard
      they go,
No matter the size
      they fit just fine,
All the items
      will stow.

This is the age
      there is no logic,
Of what should be kept
      or not,
All the things
      are welcomed in,
Finding
      their own spot,
Rarely do
      we take things out,
To make some room
      for more,
Or be more selective
      in what's brought home,
And put behind
      the door.

Some things are loved
      and some are not,
But to later use
      we think,
It's getting packed
      a bit too cramped,
Being filled up
      to the brink,
We merely try
      to fold more neatly,
The things
      that we have stored,
So we can
      at a future time,
Add
      to the building hoard.

A moment comes
      to most of us,
When
      we take a pause,
Looking at
      our cluttered space,
And wonder
      what's the cause,
This time to review
      of what we have,
Acknowledging
      all that's collected,
Keeping those things
      that make our hearts sing,
And revisiting
      all the neglected.

Decisions to
  release certain things,
May at first
  seem entirely daunting,
Yet those are the pieces
  weighing us down,
We need sweet release
  from their haunting,
The thinning out time
  for those you see,
Is the age
  of genuine knowing,
That things are not
  merely just things,
It's a sign that your soul
  is growing.

I HAVE TWELVE CATS

My cat is black
      my cat is white,

My cat is loud
      and likes to fight,

My cat is short
      my cat is small,

My cat is silly
      and likes to crawl,

My cat is soft
      my cat is quick,

My cat is frisky
      and likes to lick,

My cat is strange
      my cat is fun,

I have twelve cats
      rolled into one.

RIPPLES

I sit on the edge,

My feet dangle down,

Dip a toe in,

It makes not a sound,

Ripples start small,

Moving outward each ring,

Who will they touch?

What shifts will they bring?

MY SISTER'S TOES

My sister's toes
      crave to be free,
Fresh air to breathe
      and daylight to see,

Her piggies don't like
      to be wrapped up in socks,
Like an ice hockey jock
      in a penalty box,

Sandals and flip flops
      pass the test,
Sneakers are what
      make her toes feel stressed,

Spring and summer
      are no problem at all,
The issues arise
      when we move into fall,

As weather turns colder
      our mother insists,
That her toes be covered
      and not with her fists,

Fight as they do
      clean socks are required,
As for our family
      we're all pretty tired,

Her toes are quite stubborn
    making life difficult,
A house in chaos
    is the result,

Her face is wild
    in her hands she does cup,
Those ten little toes
    that I wish would grow up.

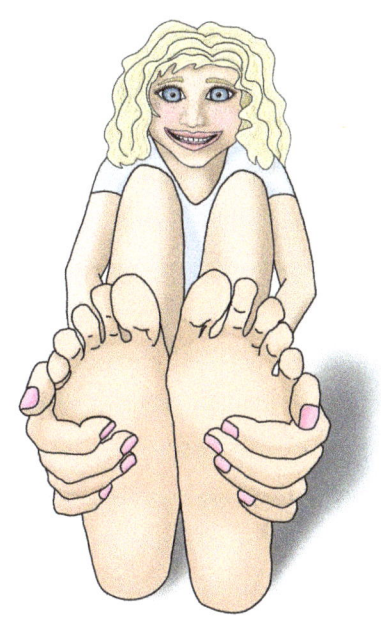

THUNDEROUS BEAST

We have a monster
      who jumps in our home,

He does seem to wander
      he does seem to roam,

He shakes the house
      several times each day,

And while I am sleeping
      he comes out to play,

He rattles the ceiling
      he rattles the floors,

He rattles the windows
      he rattles the doors,

I have yet to lay eyes
      on this thunderous beast,

For that I am thankful
      to say in the least,

Our home is quite quiet
      more often than not,

The street ends abruptly
      at the front of our lot,

To the left of our home
      stands a fence made of chain,

Right next to that
      runs the monorail train.

MORE

All grown up,

With no time to play,

Snore all night,

And work all day.

Coffee to sip,

As you run out the door,

So me and the rest,

Can have a bit more.

THE TRAVEL OF TIME

Some times are good
        some times are great,

But time always moves
        in circles not straight,

The travel of time
        is all relative,

The speed that it moves
        appears selective,

While doing the things
        that you don't want to do,

Hoping those times
        are far and are few,

It stands almost still
        barley moving at all,

Creeping so slowly
>	advancements so small,

When spirits are high
>	it moves very fast,

These are the times
>	that minutes don't last,

As you get older
>	it picks up the pace,

Time running out
>	near the end of the race,

Savor all moments
>	recall what you've seen,

But live in the now
>	not the space in between.

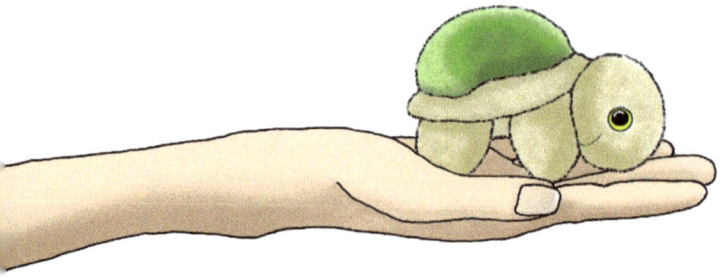

TURTLE

My turtle is small,
He fits in my palm,
A sweet little creature,
He's slow and he's calm.

Given to me,
A pet like no other,
He also has needs,
I try not to smother.

The comfort I find,
When I hold him tight,
Makes me feel good,
Makes me feel light.

He fits in my pocket,
And sleeps in my bed,
He never gets wet,
And never gets fed.

His mouth is sewn shut,
He has two plastic eyes,
But when I'm upset,
He shares in my cries.

His insides are stuffed,
His outsides are woolly,
With all of my heart,
I couldn't love him more fully.

SEARCHING FOR ME

I look left - I look up,

I look right - I look down,

I am searching for me,

Like a spring that is wound,

Through tender reflection,

I am able to see,

It's my choice to bring forth,

The best version of me.

LIVE IN THE PRESENT

It's good to be little,

It's fun to be small,

With bright imaginations,

Not yet closed to it all,

You are able to see,

With clear eyes wide,

If you muster the courage,

Where the fairies do hide,

Go play in the sunshine,

Go play in the light,

Filled with curiosity,

Befriend that winged sprite,

For moments pass quickly,

They won't be repeated,

If you live in the present,

You will never feel cheated.

NUMBERED PARTS

From his mind
        it takes its form,
From his sweat
        and hands well worn,

Package opened
        all pieces there,
Instructions read
        he says a prayer,

With courage up
        not faint of heart,
He knows there isn't
        one extra part,

An Allen wrench
        comes in a bag,
This is easy
        he wants to brag,

Nuts and bolts
        and numbered parts,
Metal washers
        and two false starts,

Steps four through six
        he must repeat,
Finally, now
        it is complete,

Stepping back
        a breath he drew,
Looking down
        at the unused screw.

CHARADES

The grass is so high,
It tickles the sky,

She bends back the blades,
Seeing through the charades,

Gaming played all around,
So she picks safer ground,

Her time will come after much learning,
When she'll join in and stop her observing.

BOO BEAR

My first name is Boo
      and my last name is Bear,

Covered in chenille
      never had any hair,

Hauled all around
      rubbed thin in some places,

We sleep together tight
      touching our faces,

Pale yellow in color
      with black thread eyes,

That see your distress
      when we say quick goodbyes,

I sit right here
      all night and all day,

Just where you left me
      keeping monsters at bay,

Your heart beats strong
> mine's filled with white fluff,

We smile at each other
> and hug when life's tough,

You will grow up
> we've made quite a pair,

And I'll stay the same
> no worse for the wear.

PETITE

Her nose is small,

Though the end still grows,

Her feet are petite,

But look at those toes!

Adored by all,

She leads the parade,

Inside we're the same,

So be not afraid.

TINY HOUSE

Our house is so cramped
      it's tiny inside,

We barely all fit
      not one place to hide,

The ceiling is low
      the windows are small,

Doors must be closed
      or they'll block off the hall,

We take turns eating
      only two at the table,

Plates so small
      barley fitting a bagel,

Our house is packed tight
      we can't fit any more,

We share it with love
      filled ceiling to floor.

DO YOU SEE?

Do you see
      what is not there?
What others can't
      or do not dare,
Are there wisps
      of light and love,
Sent to you
      from far above,
Ground yourself
      and open up,
Accept your gifts
      and fill your cup,
You are here
      to learn and grow,
Let the forces
      ebb and flow,
There are some
      who may not feel,
What you do
      and try to steal,
Away your strength
      and break your will,
They need more time
      to self-fulfill,
On their path
      you let them be,
It's not their time
      to truly see.

COUNTING SHEEP

The space inside my head is dear,
All memories stored are very clear,
I pluck each out like a tiny thread,
Inspecting the new as I rest my head,
Most give me comfort I do find,
The ones that don't I leave behind,
I fill those voids with better thoughts,
Which makes me smile while connecting dots,
These times of review before I sleep,
Help me find peace to count the sheep.

ACKNOWLEDGEMENTS

Turf, although this book is dedicated to you, I would also like to acknowledge your dependability. You are my rock. Not a patient rock, but a solid one. I cannot count how many times you asked me when I was going to be finished with this book. This book is finally finished and I am already thinking about book two.

Brad, I would like to thank you for providing me with much needed tech support. I am not unintelligent, yet may appear so to some, including you. Occasionally, electrical things seem to simply enjoy playing games with me. Thank you for being available to referee.

Haley, thank you for hearing what comes out of my mouth and my mind. Your creative sounding board services are appreciated. Many people do not get me or my visions, yet you thankfully do.

Together, we make a marvelous tribe and I am grateful that all of you are in my life.

ABOUT THE AUTHOR

Susan A. Turfle lives in the Mid-Atlantic region of the USA. She has always been an inquisitive and artistic soul. Throughout her childhood, she could be found drawing and creating things out of whatever she could scrounge from around her home or outside. Taking apart her jewelry box in order to get to the wind-up movement mechanism to see how it worked and use it for more creative applications was simply what she considered to be normal behavior.

Drawing, painting, sewing, cross stitching, working in porcelain clay, writing, metalsmithing, and acid staining concrete are some pieces that contribute to making up her self-taught creative toolset. She began writing poetry over fifteen years ago but felt a very strong pull to publish in 2021.

Once she chose to share her poems, she felt compelled to share her artwork as well. She calls her original artwork "doodlestrations", which results from a merging of doodles and illustrations.

Her quirky poems and doodlestrations are for ages 2 to 102!

Interested in future books?

Follow Susan A. Turfle on social media for the latest news and new book release dates.
Also visit:

MakingRipplesPublishing.com
SusanATurfle.com

MakingRipplesPublishing.com

Made in the U.S.A.
Westminster, MD

November 2021

www.ingramcontent.com/pod-product-compliance
Lightning Source LLC
Chambersburg PA
CBHW051621010526
44119CB00009B/226